Ellie Speaks

Joan Riedel

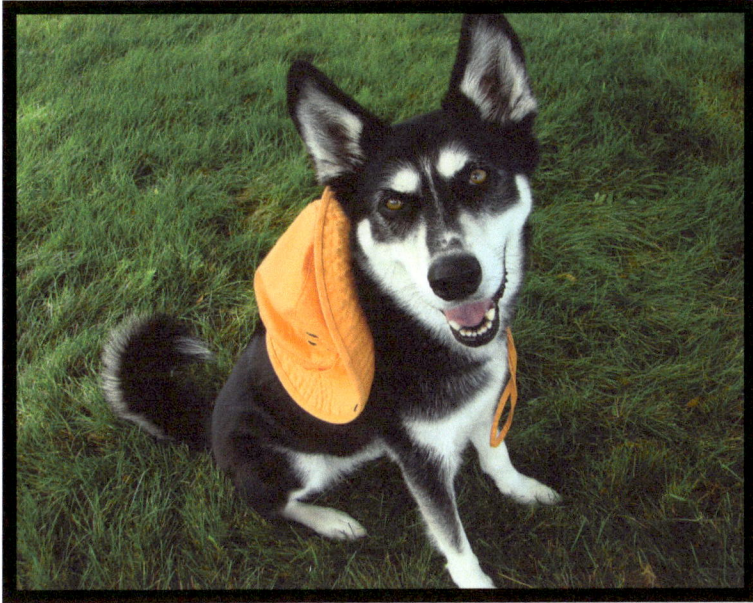

Published by Orange Hat Publishing 2015
ISBN 978-1-943331-05-5

No animals were harmed in the making of this book
. . . although occasionally they were mildly annoyed.

Orange Hat
PUBLISHING

www.orangehatpublishing.com

For Emily and Hanna

Always follow your dreams.

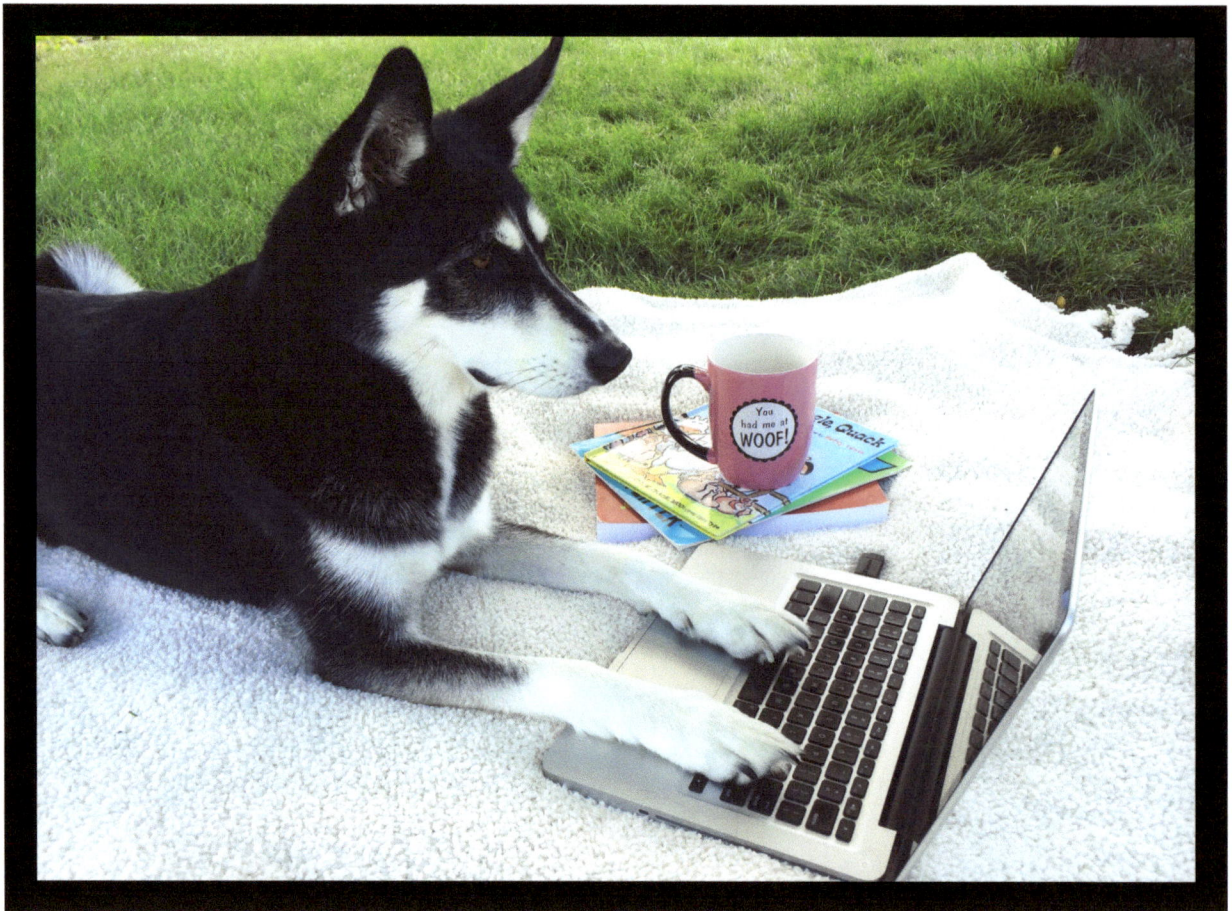

Dear Spring,

You will be arriving soon. I want you to know that you are not my first spring and you won't be my last spring, but one thing is for sure: I have been missing you since my last fall.

Love, Ellie 🐾

"It is nice finding that place where you can just go and relax."
~ Moises Arias

PAWSing to schedule my "me" time today. 🐾

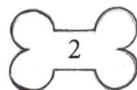

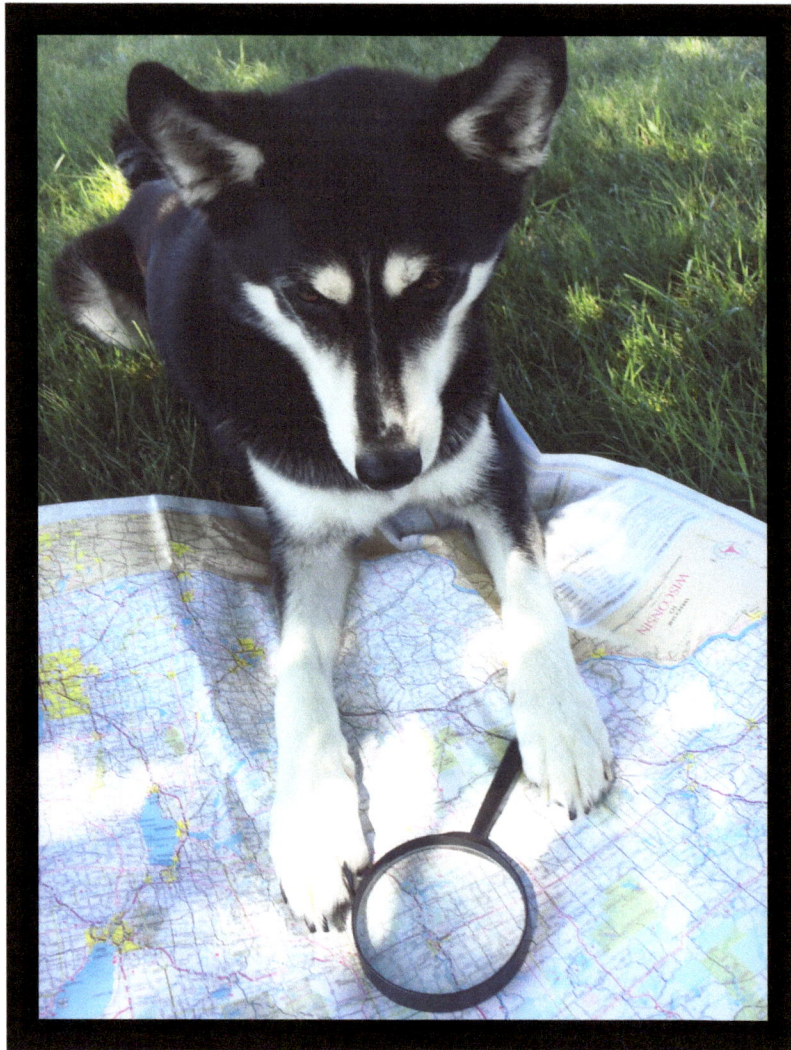

"*Map out your future, but do it in pencil. The road ahead is as long as you make it. Make it worth the trip.*"
~ *Jon Bon Jovi*

PAWSing to make sure I don't miss any stops along the way.

3

"Spring is nature's way of saying, 'Let's party!'"
~ Robin Williams

PAWSing to love spring! 🐾

"Nothing but heaven itself is better than a friend who is really a friend."
~ Plautus

PAWSing for a nap with my friend Dumpling. 🐾

5

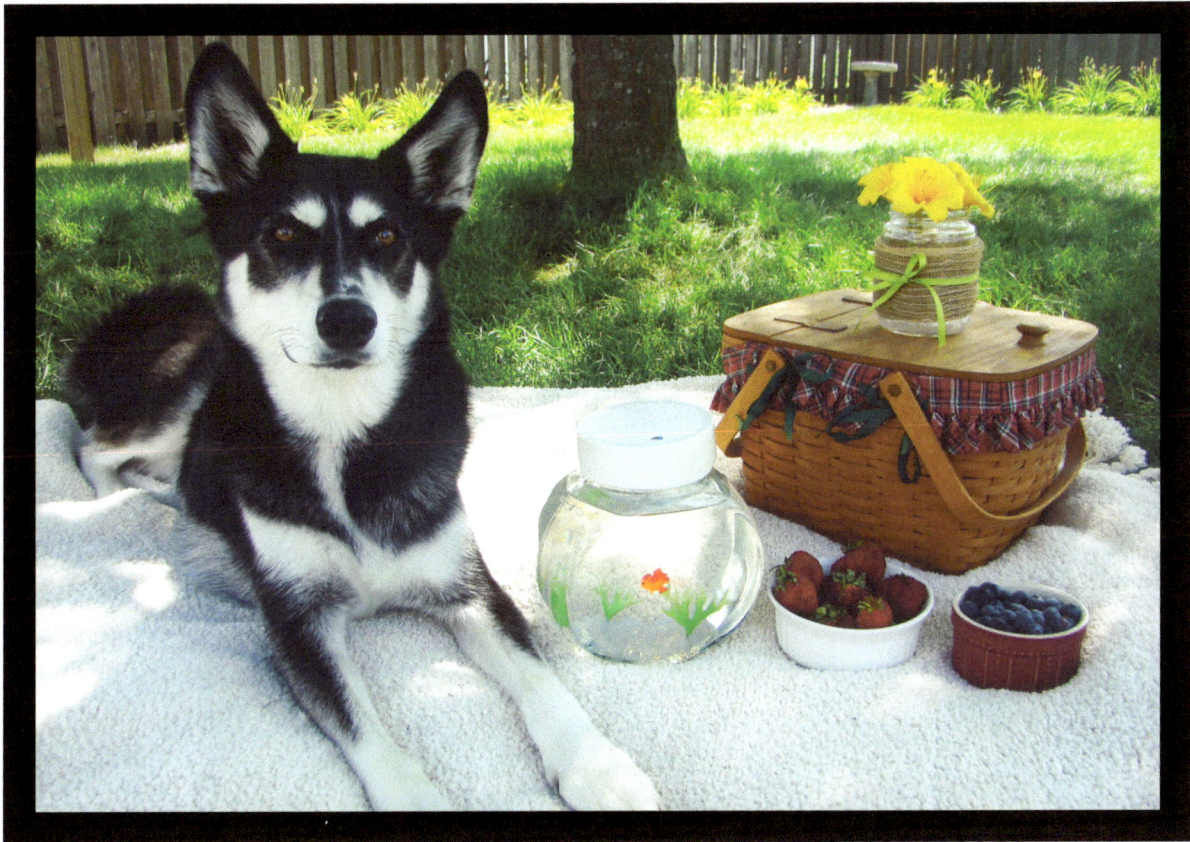

"Why did you do all this for me?" he asked. "I don't deserve it. I've never done anything for you."

"You have been my friend," replied Charlotte. "That in itself is a tremendous thing. . . ."

~ E.B. White, Charlotte's Web

PAWS and schedule friendship dates. 🐾

6

"*A hero is somebody who voluntarily walks into the unknown.*"
~ *Tom Hanks*

PAWS for a second if needed, but know that a hero is always there right inside of you.

"A best friend is like a four leaf clover, hard to find and lucky to have."
~ Sarah Jessica Parker

PAWSing to say that Irish you a happy St. Patrick's Day. 🐾

"You are never too old to set another goal or to dream a new dream."
~ C.S. Lewis

PAWSing . . . I am totally on board with that!

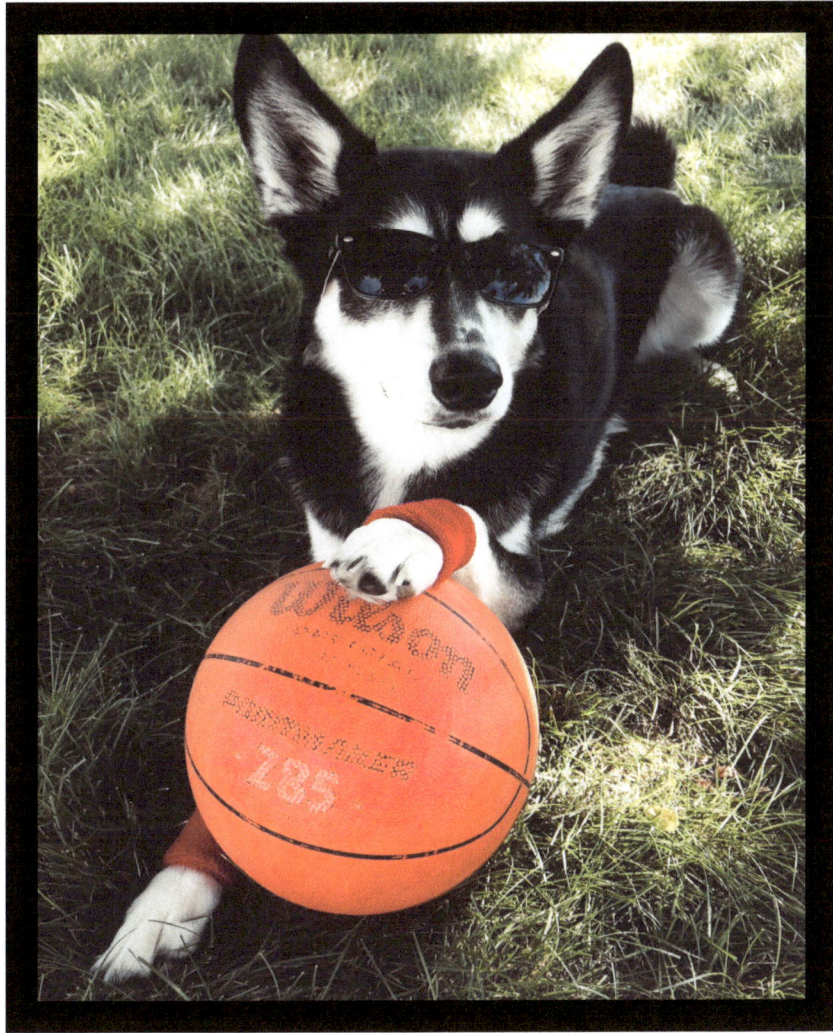

"*I always wanted to be a basketball player. Nothing more, nothing less.*"

~ Dirk Nowitzki

There will always be a personal win every time you PAWS and "assist" someone.

"A friend is a gift you give yourself."
~ Robert Louis Stevenson

PAWSing . . . Just hanging out with my favorite peeps tonight. 🐾

11

"Dear IRS,
I am writing to you to cancel my subscription. Please remove my name from your mailing list."

~ Charles M. Schulz

PAWSing . . . No, it isn't cold and flu season. Now it is tax season!

12

"The best therapist has fur and four legs."
~ Unknown

PAWSing. . . Walk-ins welcome! open 24/7. free visits, but Milk-Bone donations are gladly accepted. 🐾

"The amount of sleep required by the average person is five minutes more."
~ Wilson Mizener

PAWSing to sponsor this product. The tag says it's a sleeping bag. Sure enough, 100% of the time it works. I climb in and fall asleep! 🐾

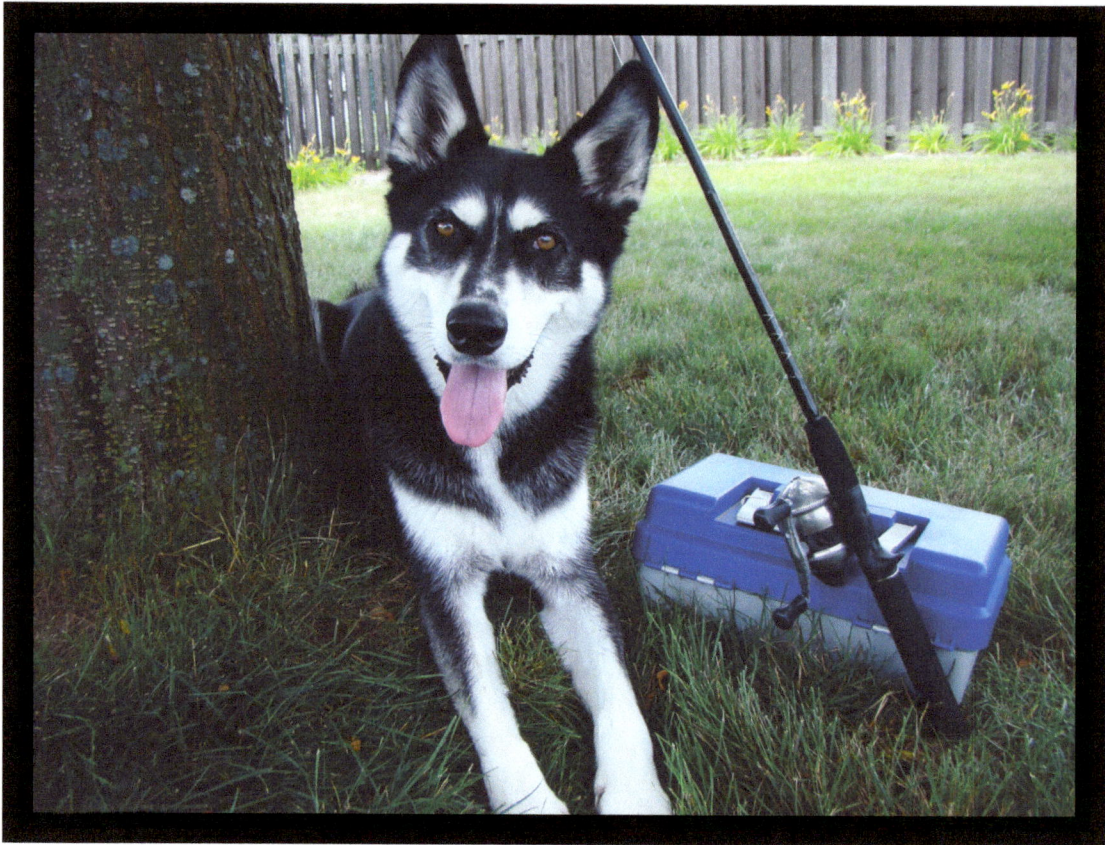

"I only fish on days that end with a y."
~ Unknown

PAWSing . . . I know I am going to have a "reel" good time today!

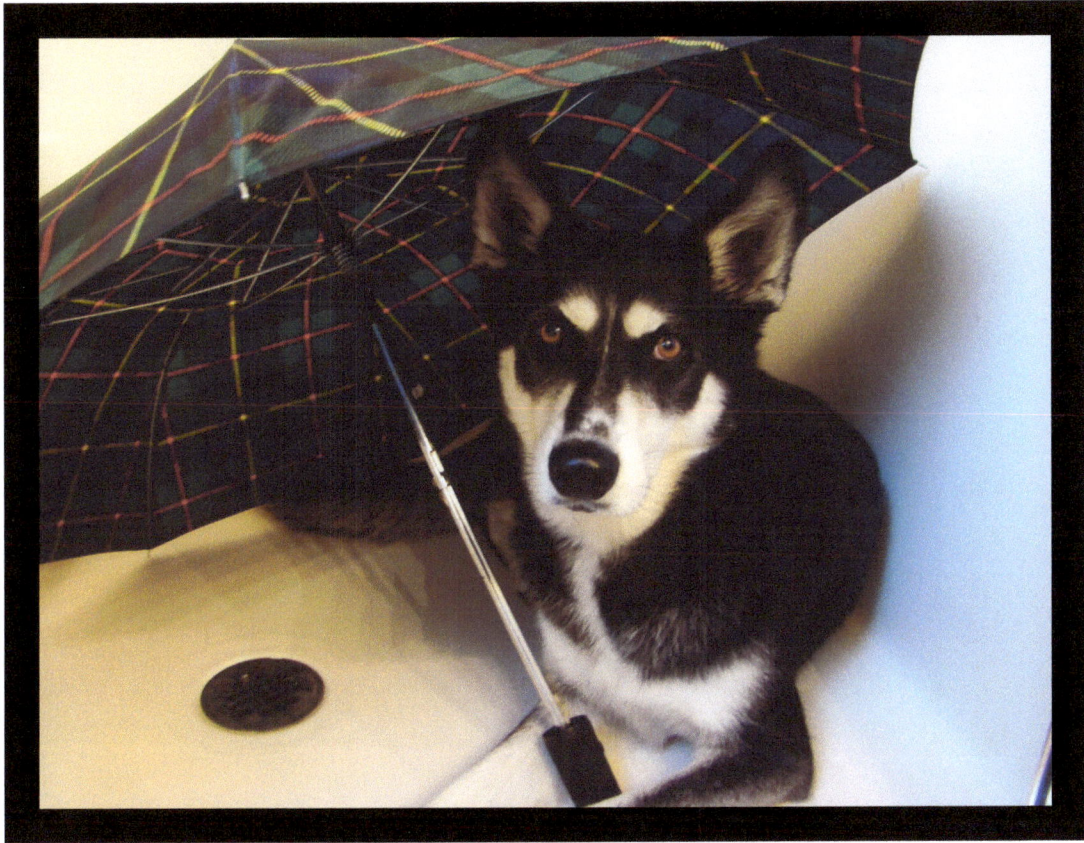

"Sometimes, I wish that I was the weather. You'd bring me up in conversation forever. And when it rained, I'd be the talk of the day."
~ John Mayer

PAWsing . . . So happy I already have my walk in for today. I heard that there is a strong possibility of a shower later today. 🐾

"Baby it's cold outside."
~ *Frank Loesser*

PAWSing to make sure I have everything . . .
Hat ✓
Mittens ✓
Sweater ✓
Boots ✓
Sense of humor ✓ 🐾

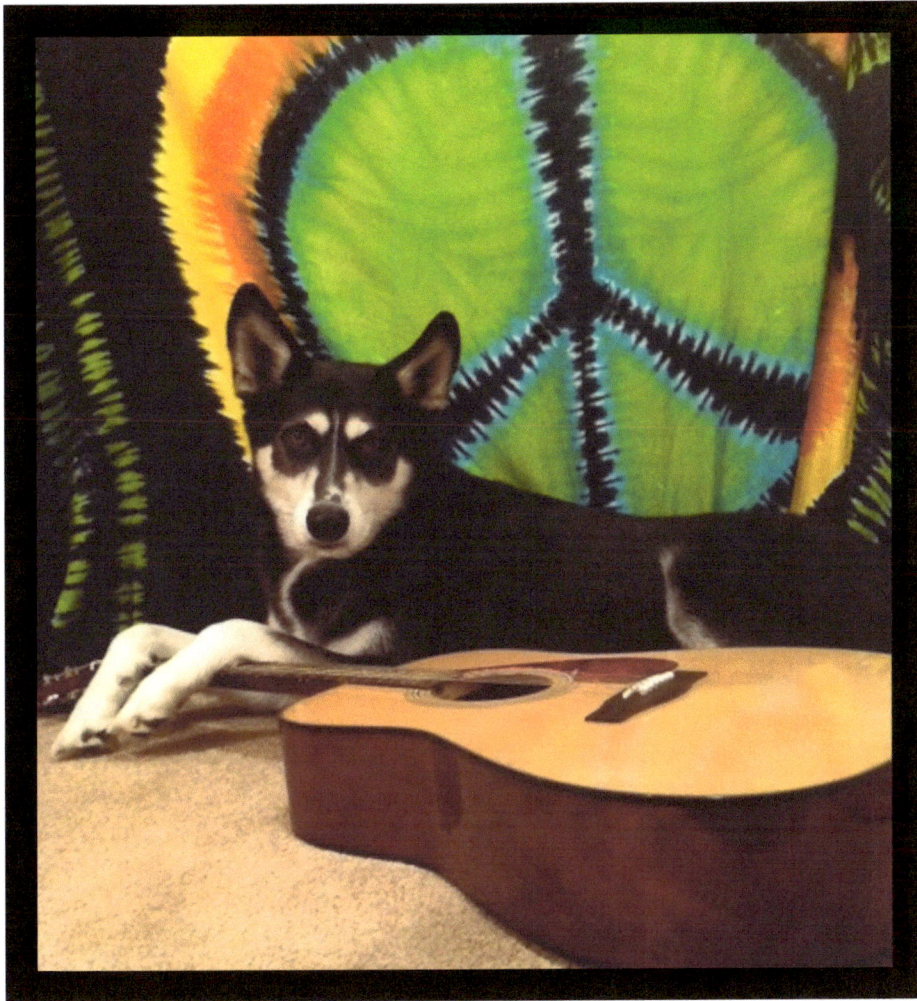

"Music is life. That's why our hearts have beats."
~ Unknown

PAWSing . . . I'm feeling the beat today. 🐾

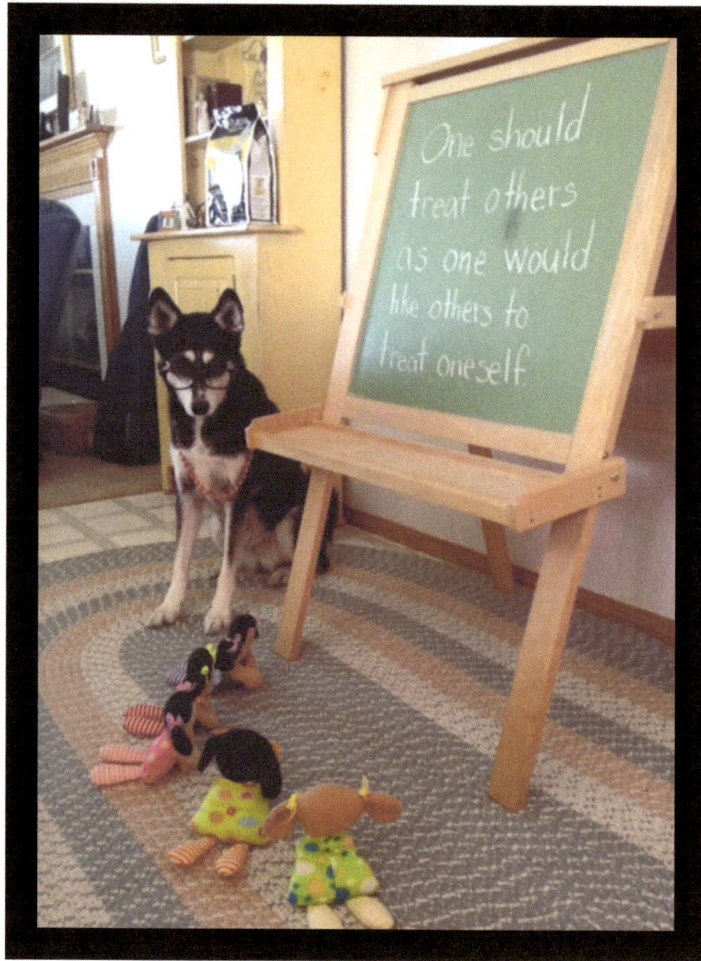

"Do not fill their heads with fluff. Teach children the most important things they need to learn."

~ Joan Riedel

PAWSing to teach the Golden Rule.

19

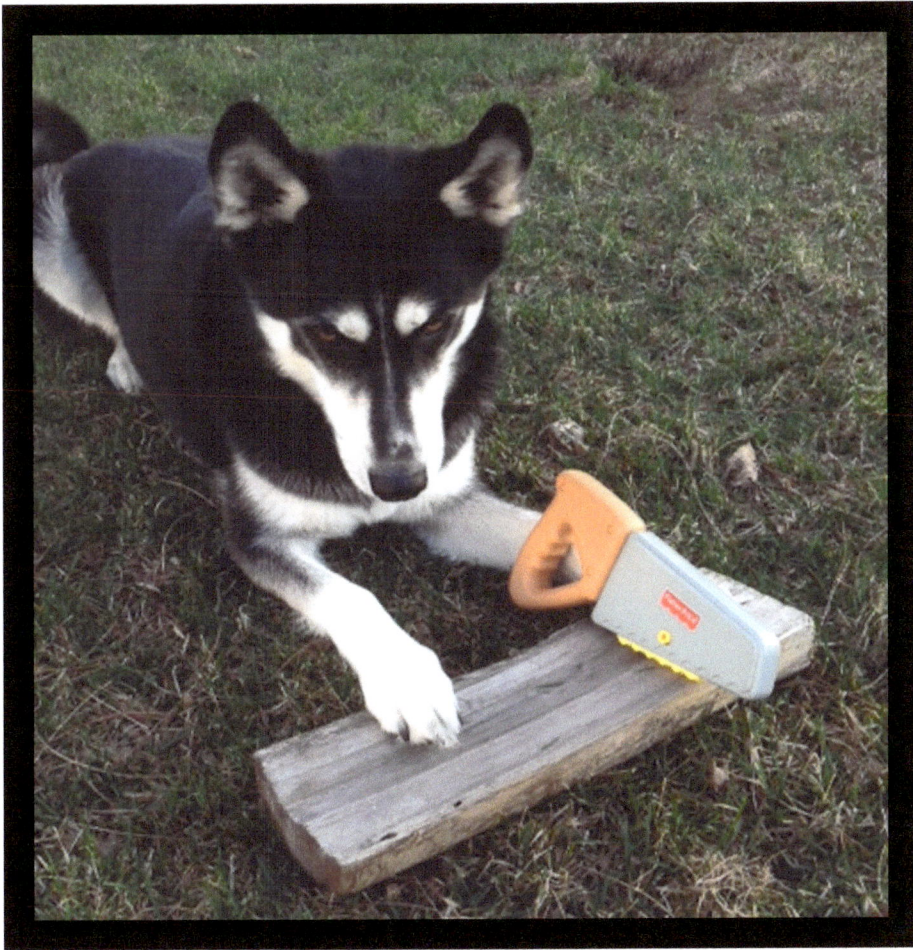

"I'm so good at sleeping I can do it with my eyes closed."
~ Unknown

PAWSing . . . Almost finished! Everyone thought I was sound asleep last night. Turns out I was just sawing logs. 🐾

"Always be yourself! Unless you can be Batman. Then always be Batman."
~ Unknown

PAWSing . . . Every once in a while I get this feeling that I just may be Batman.

21

"Just once I'd like to wake up, turn on the news, and hear, 'Monday morning has been cancelled. Go back to sleep.'"
~ Unknown

PAWSing . . . Hello? Is that you, Early Monday Morning? Let me introduce you to Hit Snooze Button. 🐾

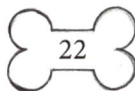

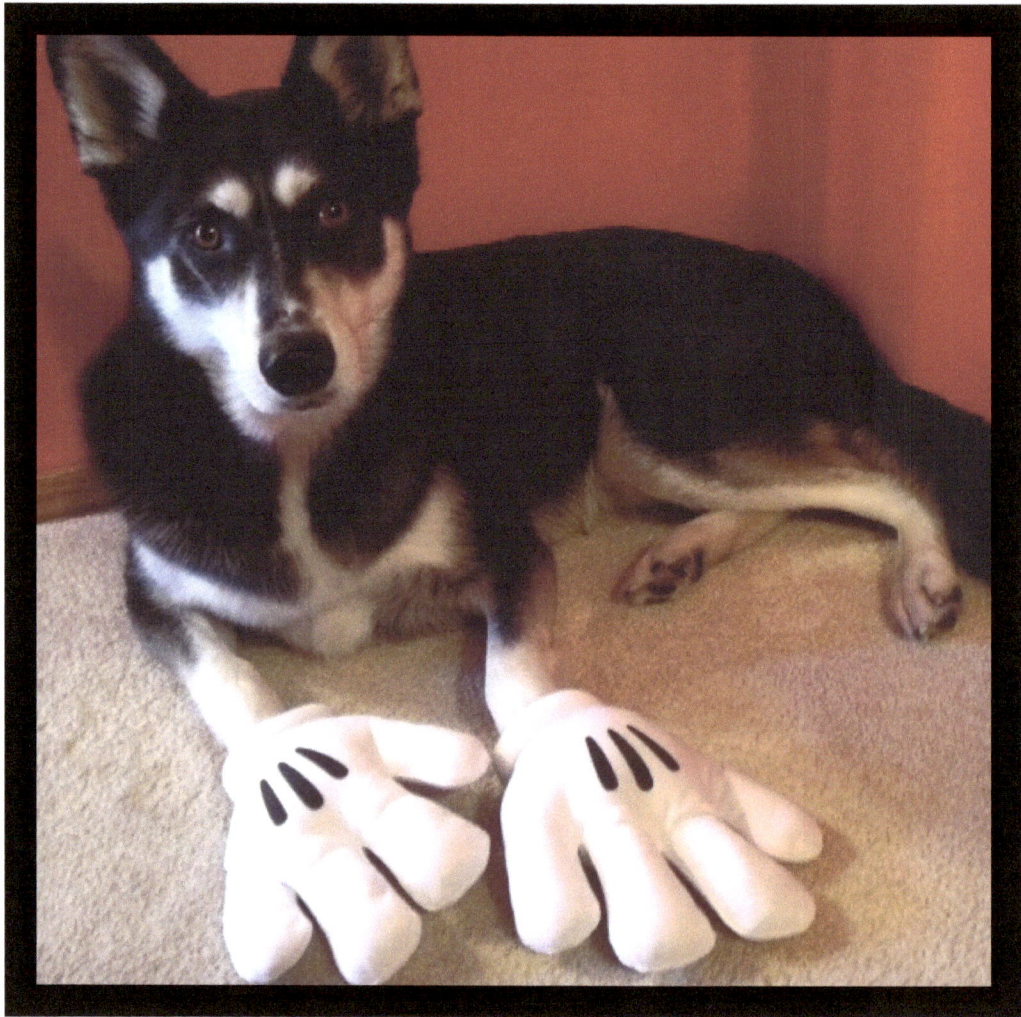

"*I only hope that we don't lose sight of one thing—that it was all started by a mouse.*"

~ *Walt Disney*

PAWSing . . . Imagine that! 🐾

23

"Connect with something greater than yourself."
~ Unknown

PAWSing to reconnect with nature. 🐾

24

"If your ship doesn't come in, swim out to it!"
~ Jonathan Winters

PAWSing . . . Good thing I can dog paddle! 🐾

"What counts isn't the frame, it's what you put in it."
~ Otto Preminger

PAWSing . . . I think I was framed. 🐾